AND I LOVE YOU, GOD.

By Ruthann Barrie

WestBow Press books may be ordered through booksellers or by contacting:

WestBow Press
A Division of Thomas Nelson
1663 Liberty Drive
Bloomington, IN 47403
www.westbowpress.com
1-(866) 928-1240

Because of the dynamic nature of the Internet, any web addresses or links contained in this book may have changed since publication and may no longer be valid. The views expressed in this work are solely those of the author and do not necessarily reflect the views of the publisher, and the publisher hereby disclaims any responsibility for them.

Any people depicted in stock imagery provided by Thinkstock are models, and such images are being used for illustrative purposes only. Certain stock imagery © Thinkstock.

ISBN: 978-1-4497-7851-4 (e)
ISBN: 978-1-4497-7850-7 (sc)

Library of Congress Control Number: 2012923045

Printed in the United States of America

WestBow Press rev. date: 12/13/2012

WestBow
PRESS
A DIVISION OF THOMAS NELSON

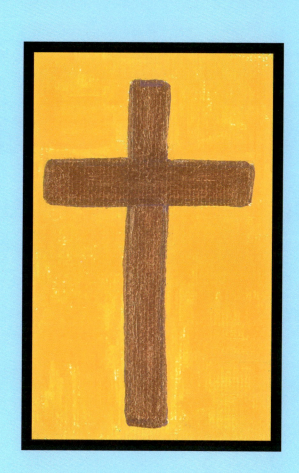

When I come you will see;
there is no One like Me.

I have made you.

I can lead you.

All you have comes from Me.

PLAY
AIR
SUNSHINE
WATER
GOD
LOVE
FOOD
WORK
GOD'S LOVE
CLOTHING
PEACE

I can save you. I can heal you.
There is no One like Me.

Teach the children how to know
Me, so they'll see as they grow;

That I join them in their hearts
and will never let them go.

There is no one, no one, no one like you. You are precious, you are special. There is no child like you.

I love you always and I will always stay. I Am Jesus and I Am the only way.

I can take you up to heaven to live with Me in joy and peace. Don't let prayer ever be ended, closeness is what I've intended. Be My child, choose, be My child. For there is no one like Me.

Dear Jesus, thank you for dying on the cross and rising again so my sins can be forgiven. I'm sorry for my sins and I make You the Lord of my life. Thank you, God; Father, Son, and Holy Spirit, one God. I want to live with You in joy and peace. Amen.

CPSIA information can be obtained
at www.ICGtesting.com
Printed in the USA
LVIC052047030113

314277LV00002B